Original title:
The Winding Road

Copyright © 2024 Creative Arts Management OÜ
All rights reserved.

Author: Wyatt Kensington
ISBN HARDBACK: 978-9916-90-826-6
ISBN PAPERBACK: 978-9916-90-827-3

Bends in Time

Whispers drift on autumn air,
Moments fold, a silent prayer.
Echoes shift like shadows cast,
We chase the dreams of futures past.

Time entwined, a waltz of fate,
Each bend reveals what we create.
Past and present softly weep,
In the heart's depths, secrets keep.

Flowing Through the Infinite

Stars alight in endless skies,
Waves of time, no goodbye lies.
Currents pull, a cosmic song,
In the flow, we all belong.

Galaxies dance in silent grace,
Infinite realms, a vast embrace.
Journey forth without a map,
In the flow, we find our path.

Arc of Discovery

Curved horizons stretch and bend,
Every turn, a twist, a friend.
Through the fog, our visions clear,
In the quest, we lose our fear.

Each step taken, heart awake,
Unseen bonds begin to break.
In this journey, truth resides,
With each arc, adventure guides.

Veils of the Past

Shadows linger, soft and light,
Whispers trace the edges bright.
Veils of yore, they gently sway,
Hiding truths from yesterday.

In the layers, secrets lie,
Echoes of a silent cry.
Unraveling, we start to see,
The veils that bind, our history.

Beyond Each Turn

The road unfolds, a mystery bright,
With whispers of dreams in the soft light.
Each corner hides a tale yet to tell,
Where hope and wonder in shadows dwell.

The sky stretches wide, endless and clear,
As paths intertwine, drawing us near.
With every step, a heartbeat so true,
Beyond each turn lies something new.

Twilight on the Path

The sun dips low, painting skies in gold,
As twilight casts its gentle hold.
With shadows dancing on the ground,
A serene hush blankets all around.

In stillness, whispers of night begin,
As stars awaken, their lights within.
The path ahead, though dim and unclear,
Guides us with dreams that draw us near.

Rhythms of the Journey

Every step echoes a silent song,
A melody where we all belong.
With each heartbeat, the journey unfolds,
In laughter and tears, our story holds.

The rhythm of life flows soft yet strong,
Carrying dreams where we weave along.
With feet on the ground, but hearts set free,
We dance to the pulse of our own symphony.

The Symmetry of Steps

In the dance of life, we find our place,
Each step a rhythm, a gentle grace.
With balance found in the ebb and flow,
We learn to trust where the currents go.

The path is a canvas, painted by time,
In every story, a reason to climb.
As we move forward, hand in hand,
We find the beauty in each grain of sand.

Shadows of Tomorrow

In whispers soft, the shadows creep,
Dancing lightly where dreams sleep.
A future bright, yet cloaked in gray,
   Awaits the dawn of a new day.

Each step we take, a choice unveils,
A journey marked by silent trails.
With hope as guide and love as light,
Together we'll face the encroaching night.

Routes Beneath Starlit Skies

Beneath the cloak of twilight's glow,
Endless paths where wanderers go.
With every star, a story spun,
In the night's embrace, we become one.

The constellations whisper low,
Guiding hearts that yearn to flow.
Each route a promise, bright and true,
Under the watchful skies of blue.

Descent into Unsung Valleys

Into the depths where silence sings,
A world unknown, where sorrow clings.
Valleys deep where few have tread,
Among the shadows, dreams are fed.

Each echo holds a story old,
Of hearts once brave, of spirits bold.
In every sigh, a tale unfolds,
Of hopes reborn and love retold.

Crossing Paths with Fate

In moments brief, our lives entwine,
A fate so fierce, a dance divine.
With every glance, a spark ignites,
Transforming shadows into lights.

Our hearts collide in cosmic play,
As time and chance pave the way.
With open arms, we brave the fall,
Embracing what has brought us all.

Curves Beneath the Sky

The sun dips low, a golden hue,
Clouds drift gently, painted blue.
Mountains rise, their shadows long,
Nature sings a timeless song.

Rivers twist through valleys wide,
Where dreams and currents coincide.
Breezes dance on fields of green,
In this realm, peace is serene.

Stars awaken, a twinkling sight,
Guiding souls through the night.
Whispers float on twilight air,
Curves beneath the sky, so rare.

Echoes of the Unknown

In silent woods, where shadows play,
Echoes call from far away.
Murmurs wrapped in mystery,
Deep within the ancient trees.

Footsteps tread on paths of lore,
Voices linger, evermore.
Every rustle speaks a tale,
As twilight drapes its woven veil.

The heartbeat of the earth resounds,
In mysteries that know no bounds.
Lost in thoughts, we roam, we seek,
The echoes whisper, soft but bleak.

Meandering Dreams

Beneath the surface, currents flow,
Casting visions soft and slow.
In the twilight, shadows blend,
Where dreams begin and never end.

Moonlit paths, a guiding light,
Leading hearts through starry night.
Floating thoughts like paper boats,
In a sea where time uncoats.

Strangers met in fleeting glances,
In these dreams, the spirit dances.
With each step, we break the seams,
Of waking life, our meandering dreams.

Whispers Through the Trees

Among the branches, secrets dwell,
Leaves tell stories, soft and swell.
Gentle rustles on the breeze,
Carrying whispers through the trees.

Nature's breath, a lullaby,
Swaying softly, nigh and nigh.
Every tickle of the vines,
Holds the heart where stillness shines.

In the grove where shadows wane,
Mysteries entwined with the rain.
Speak to me, oh ancient wood,
In every whisper, I feel good.

Shadows Dance in Twists

In the twilight, shadows play,
They weave and turn, they sway.
Whispers of the fading light,
Chasing dreams into the night.

Beneath the trees, they spin around,
Soft echoes of a muted sound.
Laughter lingers, sweet and low,
As stars emerge, the shadows glow.

With this dance, the night unfolds,
Stories told in hues of gold.
Every twist a tale to share,
In the silence, magic's there.

As dawn approaches, shadows wane,
Yet memories remain the same.
In every heart, their steps reside,
A timeless waltz, where dreams abide.

Serpentine Dreams

In the depths of slumber's hold,
Whispers of the night unfold.
Serpentine paths, so gently sway,
Guiding thoughts as night turns gray.

Curled around a silver moon,
Dreams awaken, soft as June.
With every twist, they ebb and flow,
Fleeting moments, fragile glow.

Through the valleys of the mind,
Winding trails to seek and find.
In this dance of night's embrace,
Hope ignites in every space.

When morning breaks, the dreams will fade,
But in our hearts, they are laid.
Serpentine, they linger near,
In shadows deep, they reappear.

Curved Horizons

Golden sun meets azure skies,
Curved horizons where beauty lies.
With every breath of morning's breeze,
Nature's whispers bring us ease.

Mountains rise, and valleys bend,
Winding paths that never end.
Each turn a promise, bright and clear,
To chase the dreams we hold so dear.

Clouds drift softly, shadows play,
Painting skies in hues of gray.
Underneath, the world will bloom,
In every corner, life and room.

As day gives way to twilight's glow,
Curved horizons start to show.
In the dusk, we find our sight,
Beyond the curve, awaits the light.

Where the Trail Leads

Step by step, we find our way,
On a trail through night and day.
With every turn, a tale unfolds,
A journey filled with dreams and gold.

Through the forest, whispers call,
Leaves will rustle, shadows fall.
Guided by the light above,
Each footfall tells of hope and love.

Cross the river, climb the hills,
Every moment, heart it fills.
Where the trail leads, we shall go,
Facing the winds, embracing flow.

At the end, we'll look behind,
The path we've walked, the truths we find.
In the journey lies the deed,
Where the trail leads, we are freed.

Echoing Footsteps Forward

In the stillness of the night,
Footsteps echo through the dark,
Each one bringing dreams to light,
Years of hope, a single spark.

With every step, the future calls,
Whispers carried by the breeze,
Breaking through the ancient walls,
Chasing shadows, setting free.

A journey paved with hopes anew,
Footprints left upon the way,
Every choice a chance to view,
What tomorrow's skies will say.

With every turn and every bend,
Echoes whisper lessons learned,
In the night, we find a friend,
As from darkness, dawn returned.

Twists of Fate

In the dance of time and chance,
Life presents its fickle game,
Moments shift, a strange romance,
Paths diverge, yet hearts remain.

A whispered secret in the air,
Brings together strangers lost,
Through fortune's whim, we come to share,
Laughter born from bitter frost.

With every detour, wisdom grows,
Lessons learned through joy and pain,
Embrace the path where the river flows,
For fate's designs are never plain.

As tides shift with the moon's embrace,
We navigate the highs and lows,
In the twists, we find our grace,
And through it all, the heart still knows.

Journey's Embrace

Underneath a starry dome,
Wanderers seek their destined place,
With every step, they leave their home,
In the world's vast, warm embrace.

Mountains high and valleys low,
Every path a story told,
Find the strength to let love grow,
As life's adventures unfold.

Through winding roads and rivers wide,
Nature sings a timeless song,
With each turn, let hope abide,
For in the journey, we belong.

As dawn awakens, hearts will soar,
With dreams ignited by the light,
Embrace the road, forevermore,
In every day, in every night.

Paths Unfolding

In shadows deep, the signs appear,
Every choice a path defined,
With whispers soft, the heart will steer,
Finding treasures intertwined.

Beneath the branches, stories breathe,
Each one marked by joy and strife,
The roots of hope, the leaves of grief,
All weave together, this is life.

With every dawn, a chance to change,
To step into the unknown bright,
The world awaits, its hands exchange,
Guiding dreams with gentle light.

As paths unfold, our hearts ignite,
We dance between the wild and free,
In every moment, pure delight,
Together on this journey, we.

Landscapes of Change

Rolling hills shift with the breeze,
Colors blend as the sun sets,
Whispers of autumn through the trees,
Nature's canvas, with no regrets.

Rivers carve tales on worn stone,
Mountains stand tall, proud and grand,
Seasons dance, we're not alone,
Beauty reigns across this land.

Clouds gather, storms might arise,
Yet after the rain comes the glow,
Each moment fleeting, like fireflies,
A cycle we cherish, we know.

In the quiet, we find our peace,
Time flows like water in streams,
With every breath, may worries cease,
In landscapes of change, we chase dreams.

Horizons Drawn

A skyline painted with twilight hues,
Promises beckon from realms afar,
Footprints trace paths of hopeful views,
Where desires meet the evening star.

The ocean's edge calls with gentle waves,
Seagulls glide on whispers of the wind,
Hearts of explorers, daring and brave,
Seek horizons where journeys begin.

Mountains loom, their peaks kissed by light,
Breathless views make spirits soar,
Every climb is a test of might,
In the distance, we find what we're for.

From valleys deep to the skies above,
Horizons drawn with strokes of fate,
Guided by the flame of love,
Every sunset, a newfound gate.

Roadside Reveries

Worn tires roll on a winding path,
Fields of gold stretch far and wide,
Moments linger in nature's math,
   Simple joys we cannot hide.

Dandelions dance with the breeze,
   Butterflies flit without a care,
Memories bloom beneath the trees,
   In roadside reveries, time is rare.

Sunshine warms the weathered stone,
   Old fences tell of days gone by,
Each mile brings a breath of home,
   Under the vast, embracing sky.

With every turn, a story's told,
A journey rich with laughter and tears,
In the heart, these moments unfold,
   Roadside reveries calm our fears.

Where Time Loops

In the echo of ages past,
Whispers linger in the air,
Every laugh, every shadow cast,
Threads of memory everywhere.

Fleeting hours in a silent dance,
Repeat like waves upon the shore,
Inviting hearts to take a chance,
In the moments we can't ignore.

Old clocks tick in rhythm's sway,
Time bends with every fleeting sigh,
In corners where children play,
Fleeting joys refuse to die.

Where time loops, we find our place,
In the stillness, a gentle tune,
Every heartbeat leaves its trace,
Beneath the watchful, silver moon.

The Long and Winding Path

The path ahead is tangled still,
With twists and turns that test the will.
Each step I take, a story grows,
Through sunlit days and moonlit shows.

The whispering winds call out my name,
As shadows dance, and paths reclaim.
Through valleys low and mountains high,
I wander forth, beneath the sky.

Each marker tells of battles fought,
Of dreams once lost and wisdom sought.
With every curve, I find my way,
The winding path will guide my day.

In Search of Light

In darkness deep, my heart will seek,
A glimmer bright, a voice to speak.
Through nights so long, I chase the dawn,
With hope my guide, I journey on.

The stars above, they flicker tight,
In every shadow, there's a light.
I'll follow paths both strange and new,
For every step brings insight true.

When doubts may rise, I'll hold the flame,
In search of light, I'll stake my claim.
With open eyes and spirit wide,
The dawn will come, my faithful guide.

Through Curves and Corners

Through curves and corners, life does weave,
A tapestry of dreams to cleave.
With every turn, I learn to bend,
Life's road is long, but not the end.

The journey twists like rivers flow,
With laughter shared and tears that glow.
Each corner turned, a lesson learned,
With each new sight, my heart is burned.

In sun and rain, I forge ahead,
Embracing all, no need for dread.
As shadows stretch, the path I take,
Through curves and corners, I will wake.

A Traveler's Soliloquy

Alone I walk, a traveler's tune,
Beneath the sun, beneath the moon.
With every step, a tale unfolds,
The roads I roam, the dreams I hold.

I ponder lives I've yet to meet,
The stories rich beneath my feet.
With pen in hand, I write my fate,
Each word a step toward what awaits.

A thousand voices whisper clear,
In every moment, I draw near.
The world unfolds, a vivid scene,
A traveler's heart, forever keen.

In the Quiet Turns

In the hush of twilight's grace,
Whispers dance in soft embrace.
Shadows play on cobbled stone,
In the quiet, hearts are known.

Echoes of the past resound,
Silent songs where dreams are found.
With each breath, a tale unfolds,
In the quiet, truth beholds.

Stars awaken, light the way,
Guiding souls who dare to stay.
Night's embrace, a tender sigh,
In the quiet, spirits fly.

Ramble and Roam

Through the fields where wildflowers sway,
I ramble free, come what may.
With every step, the world unfolds,
Tales of life and joy retold.

Winding paths through forest deep,
Secrets hidden, dreams to keep.
I roam with purpose, heart untamed,
In nature's arms, forever claimed.

Mountains rise with timeless grace,
Every curve a warm embrace.
Ramble on, let worries fade,
In every heartbeat, peace is made.

Uncharted Footsteps

Upon the trail where few have been,
Uncharted steps, a world within.
With open heart, I seek the new,
Every moment, fresh as dew.

Beneath the canopy so wide,
Whispers of the ancients guide.
Curves of earth, the wild's embrace,
In uncharted paths, I find my place.

Bridges formed of dreams and light,
Charting stars in endless night.
With each footprint, a story grows,
In uncharted lands, the spirit flows.

Secrets of the Wayfarer

Beneath the stars, the traveler finds,
Secrets told by gentle winds.
In every corner of the earth,
Echoes of joy, whispers of birth.

Footsteps trace the paths of old,
Stories waiting to be told.
With each sunrise, a gift anew,
In the journey, skies so blue.

Mysteries wrapped in twilight's shawl,
In every shadow, a silent call.
The wayfarer wanders, heart so wide,
In the secrets, they abide.

The Longing Trail

Beneath the vast and starry sky,
Footsteps echo of my sighs.
Each step whispers tales untold,
As dreams and hopes begin to unfold.

The path is worn and full of bends,
Where heartache mends and spirit sends.
With every mile, the vision brightens,
A flicker of warmth as darkness lightens.

Nature's breath, a gentle guide,
Through whispering woods, where secrets hide.
The longing grows, a fire inside,
In the vastness, I will not hide.

When shadows fall and doubts set in,
I'll chase the light and let it win.
For on this trail, I am alive,
With every step, my spirit thrives.

Detours to Destiny

Life's map is drawn with cautious lines,
Yet every turn holds rare designs.
A pause here, a shift in fate,
Rerouting dreams that can't wait.

Stormy skies may greet the way,
Yet in those clouds, the sun holds sway.
Each detour paints a story new,
A vibrant path for hearts that grew.

In tangled woods, the compass sways,
But treasure thrives in winding ways.
Every misstep finds its place,
In a dance of time and space.

The journey's rich, the lessons deep,
Through twists of fate, my heart will leap.
For every route that leads astray,
Brings closer dreams I can't delay.

The Unseen Journey

In shadows cast by moonlit nights,
The road ahead hides many sights.
Though unseen paths stretch far and wide,
A whispered hope will be my guide.

With every breath, I feel the pull,
Of journeys waiting, beautiful.
The fear of change just fuels the flame,
To seek the wild, to taste the same.

Mountains rise and valleys sway,
In silence bloom the dreams we play.
With every heartbeat, I will trust,
In unknowns that create my thrust.

So let the winds of fate unwind,
I'll find the treasures left behind.
For in each step of the unknown,
A brave new world is surely sewn.

Along the Twists and Turns

Through valleys deep and peaks so high,
The road unravels, shadows lie.
Each twist will test the soul within,
But on this road, I dare begin.

With branches swaying, whispers call,
To journey forth, to risk it all.
In every turn, a choice is laid,
Where courage blooms, and fears will fade.

The path may twist, the path may wind,
But treasures golden, one can find.
With every challenge boldly faced,
Life's sweetest moments are embraced.

So here I stand, a soul set free,
Embracing all that's meant to be.
For in this journey, I will learn,
The beauty found along each turn.

Each Turn Unfolds

In the dawn's gentle grasp, we tread,
Whispers of dreams begin to flow.
Paths twist and turn, stories unsaid,
Each step a chance, a way to grow.

Hearts beat in rhythm, a dance divine,
Lessons learned in shadows cast.
Time gifts us change, a potent sign,
In each turn, our futures amassed.

With courage kindled, we face the day,
Unraveling fate in silent grace.
Embracing the journey, come what may,
Life unfolds, a vibrant embrace.

Seeking solace

In the stillness, where shadows creep,
I find my thoughts in quiet streams.
Waves of worry begin to sleep,
Searching for peace in gentle dreams.

Moments linger, a breath of time,
Nature whispers in calming tones.
Amongst the chaos, I start to climb,
Finding solace, I'm never alone.

Beneath the boughs of ancient trees,
I feel the earth breathe soft and true.
In every rustle, a sweet release,
Guiding my heart to skies so blue.

Beneath the Sky's Embrace

Under the vast and endless blue,
Clouds drift softly, tales unfold.
Dreams woven in the morning dew,
A symphony of life, bright and bold.

Stars awaken as day retreats,
Moments captured in twilight's glow.
Nature dances, the heart it beats,
Beneath the sky, our spirits flow.

In whispers of wind, secrets shared,
The moon's soft light guides every step.
In this embrace, we stand prepared,
Embracing the night, our hearts adept.

Divergent Destinies

Paths diverge as horizons stretch,
Choices laid bare, like threads of gold.
In this tapestry, we must fetch,
Stories of these lives we hold.

Each journey taken, a tale unique,
Voices echo through the years.
In whispers quiet, the brave and meek,
Divergent paths, shaped by our fears.

Hope ignites where shadows linger,
Hands reaching out for dreams once lost.
In destiny's weave, we find the finger,
Guiding us gently, despite the cost.

Stories of the Path

On winding trails where shadows dwell,
Footprints whisper, stories tell.
Each step a memory, carved in time,
Echoes of laughter, a silent rhyme.

Through forests deep, beneath the sky,
Lost in dreams as the moments fly.
Roots entwined with hopes and fears,
Tales of joy, and distant tears.

Beneath the stars, the path unfolds,
Silver threads in the night retold.
Guided by lights that softly gleam,
Every road leads to a dream.

With every turn, a lesson learned,
Through fire and frost, the spirit burned.
The journey shapes who we become,
In stories shared, we find our home.

Navigating Life's Corners

Life's corners twist, they turn and bend,
Unexpected paths, around the end.
Moments unseen, whispers in air,
Decisions made with courage rare.

With every choice, the heart will guide,
Waves of the tide, the shifting side.
Trust the compass that lies within,
Through every loss, there's more to win.

In shadows cast where fears reside,
Shimmering light we cannot hide.
Navigating through the stormy night,
Finding solace in the dawn's first light.

As days unfold, let courage rise,
With open hearts, embrace the skies.
Through every corner, we will find,
A path of love, forever kind.

Beyond the Next Curve

Beyond the curve, the horizon calls,
Adventure waits where silence falls.
Mountains whisper, rivers sing,
In every bend, new hopes take wing.

The road may twist, the journey long,
In every heartbeat, there's a song.
Breaking barriers, chasing dreams,
In unseen worlds, nothing's as it seems.

Sunset paints the canvas bright,
Every shadow kissed by light.
Embrace the unknown, let fears depart,
Find the treasure within your heart.

With every step, the future glows,
Beyond the edge, the spirit flows.
In the dance of fate, take your turn,
For in this curve, we live and learn.

The Journey Within

In the stillness, whispers grow,
The journey within helps us know.
A forest deep, a tranquil sea,
Where thoughts can wander, free and free.

Through shadows cast, and doubts that rise,
The mirror shows the heart's true guise.
With gentle grace, self-love we find,
In every moment, a chance to unwind.

Step by step, with courage tread,
Upon the path that leads ahead.
Unlocking doors with every breath,
In the sacred dance between life and death.

As stars align in the night sky,
Listen closely; the soul's soft sigh.
In the depths of silence, wisdom speaks,
The journey within is what we seek.

Ribbons of Adventure

In forests deep where shadows creep,
Bright ribbons dance, secrets they keep.
With every step, the thrill ignites,
Unfolding paths of wondrous sights.

Mountains high, the stars align,
Across the streams of sparkling wine.
Each journey speaks, a tale untold,
In whispers soft, like threads of gold.

Beneath the skies, on wings we soar,
Embracing dreams, we ask for more.
With laughter shared, our spirits fly,
On ribbons bold, we touch the sky.

So take my hand, let's wander far,
Through every door, beneath each star.
In every turn, adventure calls,
A tapestry of life enthralls.

Trails of the Heart

In quiet woods where feelings dwell,
The trails of hearts weave tales to tell.
Each step a pulse, each breath a beat,
In nature's grace, our lives repeat.

The sun peeks through the leafy veil,
With whispers soft, it tells a tale.
In gentle streams, reflections bloom,
Emotions rise, dispelling gloom.

With every turn, connections grow,
In silent moments, love does flow.
A tapestry of souls entwined,
In heartfelt trails, our paths aligned.

So walk with me through dusk and dawn,
On trails of the heart, we journey on.
Together we'll find what's brave and true,
In every step, it leads me to you.

Horizons in Flux

At dawn's embrace, the world awakes,
Horizons shift, the earth it shakes.
With colors bright, the canvas glows,
In every change, the spirit flows.

The waves do crash, the tides will turn,
In every spark, there's much to learn.
Above, the skies paint stories vast,
In fleeting moments, wishes cast.

Through valleys deep, we seek the light,
In currents strong, we find our flight.
With hope reborn, horizons shift,
In every breath, we find the gift.

So chase the dawn, as night departs,
Explore the world, embrace the arts.
For in the flux, our dreams take shape,
In endless skies, our futures scrape.

Swaying Between Light and Dark

In twilight's glow, a dance begins,
Swaying softly, where day rescinds.
The stars emerge, a whispered spark,
The night brings peace, the shadows arc.

Amidst the trees, the whispers blend,
A harmony where hearts depend.
In every sigh, a breath of night,
Between the worlds of dark and light.

With every pulse, the moon does rise,
Casting dreams through open skies.
In gentle waves, the moments sway,
As dawn pulls near to greet the day.

So let us dance, through night and morn,
In every shade, our hearts reborn.
For life's a song, a timeless arc,
Swaying gracefully through light and dark.

Secrets of the Serpentine

In shadows deep, where whispers dwell,
A serpent glides, casting its spell.
Beneath the leaves, secrets entwined,
In silken silence, truths are confined.

A flicker of light, a glint of scale,
Mysteries offered, a whispered tale.
Twisting paths where no one strays,
In the heart of night, the serpent sways.

Landscapes of Longing

Across the valleys, dreams take flight,
Painted skies in the fading light.
Echoes of laughter float on the breeze,
In the quiet corners, my heart finds ease.

Mountains loom like giants bold,
In their shadows, stories are told.
Fields of gold, a sight to behold,
Yet longing lingers, never to fold.

Wanderlust and Winding Ways

Beneath the stars, the journey calls,
Through winding paths and silent halls.
Footprints tracing tales of old,
Adventures waiting, bold and untold.

In every corner, a story waits,
A tapestry woven by unseen fates.
With every turn, the heart will sway,
Embracing the night, come what may.

The Wayfarer's Reflection

A mirror of journeys, eyes hold the past,
Reflections of moments, shadows cast.
With every step, a lesson learned,
In the fire of time, the heart has burned.

As dawn approaches, the path grows clear,
Whispers of wisdom, the soul draws near.
In the stillness, I find my way,
The wayfarer's heart, forever will stray.

Routes of Reflection

Paths diverge in shades of green,
Whispers echo, wisdom gleaned.
Every step a tale unfolds,
In silence, secrets long held told.

Footprints softly mark the trail,
Nature sings a sweet exhale.
Amidst the trees, a pondering mind,
Finding solace, peace defined.

Rivers flow with memories past,
Time reflects in ripples cast.
Journeys charted, lessons learned,
In each heart a fire burns.

Beneath the stars, dreams take flight,
Guided by the moon's soft light.
Routes of reflection, paths anew,
In every ending, beginnings true.

A Pilgrim's Diary

Worn shoes tell of distant lands,
Pages filled with shifting sands.
Every sunrise sparks a quest,
Pilgrim's heart seeks sacred rest.

Underneath the vast blue skies,
Whispered prayers, unanswered sighs.
Mountains high, valleys deep,
In silence, dreams dare to leap.

Mapless journeys, heart as guide,
Traveling where spirits reside.
In laughter and in painful tears,
The diary bears the weight of years.

Candles lit in lonely nights,
Tracing paths by candle lights.
A pilgrim's diary, inked with grace,
Each line a step in time and space.

Journey of the Heart

With every beat, a story starts,
Navigating the maze of hearts.
Fragile bonds, both near and far,
In love's embrace, we find who we are.

Pages worn, like whispered vows,
Promises made in sacred brows.
Through storms and calms, we learn to feel,
The journey of hearts, a sacred reel.

In laughter shared and tears let flow,
Through valleys low and peaks aglow.
Moments cherished, sweet and stark,
The journey of the heart leaves its mark.

Together we weave each tangled thread,
Through all the words we left unsaid.
With open hearts, we dare to start,
A never-ending journey of the heart.

Vestiges of the Voyager

Upon the shores of time, I stand,
Traces left by a wandering hand.
Footprints etched in grains of sand,
Vestiges that speak of distant land.

In the horizon, tales unfold,
Silver linings, threads of gold.
Stars above, a compass bright,
Guiding souls through the night.

Waves embrace the stories past,
Echoes of the ship's steadfast.
In every heart, a tale remains,
Vestiges of joys and pains.

With each return, new paths to find,
In the soul, the sea entwined.
The voyager's spirit, bold and free,
Leaves vestiges for all to see.

Twists of Destiny

In shadows cast, fate spins its thread,
Paths entwined where silence led.
We dance upon the edge of dreams,
In whispered hopes, life often seems.

A glance exchanged, hearts intertwine,
Moments lost, like aged wine.
Each choice we make, a step we take,
In the tapestry, choices awake.

Through storms we walk, through light we wade,
In every turn, a bond is made.
Time weaves stories, both old and new,
In every twist, our spirits grew.

So here we stand, with open hearts,
Embracing change, where destiny starts.
From chance encounters, love will rise,
In every ending, the world complies.

Pathways Unraveled

Beneath the skies, our footsteps roam,
Each path we walk, a tale of home.
Through winding trails, each choice reveals,
The intricate dance of fate that steals.

In quiet moments, questions bloom,
What lies ahead in twilight's gloom?
Each turn, a lesson, each bend, a sign,
In the labyrinth of life, we firmly align.

The road may twist, the way unclear,
Yet courage whispers, "Keep us near."
Hand in hand, we'll face the night,
With hope as our beacon, guiding light.

The tapestry of life unfolds,
In every thread, a story told.
With every heartbeat, dreams resurrect,
Finding the treasures we don't expect.

Journey in Motion

Like rivers flow, our lives entwine,
In every bend, a twist divine.
With open hearts, we chase the sun,
This journey begun, never done.

Mountains rise, and valleys dive,
In every struggle, we learn to thrive.
Through laughter's song and sorrow's ache,
Each step we take, new paths we make.

The horizon calls, a distant shore,
In dreams we find what we're searching for.
With faith as our sail, we push through the waves,
In every heartbeat, courage saves.

Together we wander through time and space,
In every moment, we find our place.
The journey beckons, adventure waits,
With every heartbeat, destiny creates.

Footprints on Gravel

Each grain of stone, a tale of yore,
Footprints marked on the well-worn shore.
In quiet whispers, the past will tell,
Of journeys embarked, where memories dwell.

Through morning mist, we walk with grace,
In every step, we find our place.
With laughter echoing, and shadows cast,
Footprints on gravel, a link to the past.

The paths we chose, the roads we share,
Each journey taken, echoes our care.
In every footfall, history speaks,
In the dance of liveliness, the heart seeks.

So let us leave our traces here,
In every moment, hold them dear.
For as we wander, seasons change,
In footprints carved, life's beauty strange.

The Fable of Paths

In the woods where whispers lie,
Ancient trails weave low and high.
Each step a tale, a choice to make,
Through shadows deep or sunlit wake.

Time will tell where they may lead,
To valleys calm or mountains freed.
With every fork, a life is spun,
Fables told when day is done.

Winding paths of joy and pain,
Lost in laughter, found in rain.
The heart knows well which way to steer,
In the fable, we persevere.

So choose with care, each turn and bend,
For in this journey, we transcend.
A tapestry of dreams we weave,
In every moment, we believe.

Mysteries of the Direction

North and south, where do we go?
The compass spins, its dance in tow.
Secrets linger in the breeze,
Whispered softly through the trees.

Maps unfold with paths unseen,
Guiding hearts where they have been.
Across the waters, through the hills,
The mystery of direction thrills.

Stars above, they subtly guide,
In the darkness, dreams collide.
Each turn a lesson, each road a clue,
In direction's maze, we find what's true.

As we wander, let us explore,
The secrets waiting at each door.
With every step, the story grows,
In mysteries of direction, life flows.

Threads of Fate

In the loom of time, threads entwine,
Each choice a stitch, each moment divine.
Fate's gentle hand weaves tales anew,
In vibrant shades of every hue.

We find connection in the weave,
A pattern formed, we can't perceive.
Interlaced lives, a grand design,
In threads of fate, our hearts align.

Tug at one, the others sway,
The choices made guide our way.
In every twist, a bond is forged,
In threads of fate, our lives are gorged.

So let us honor this sacred thread,
Embrace the journey where we've led.
For in this tapestry, we find our place,
In the threads of fate, love leaves its trace.

Glimmers in the Turns

On winding roads where secrets gleam,
Glimmers spark in the twilight dream.
Each bend a promise, each curve a chance,
In the turns of life, we learn to dance.

Sunbeams flicker through the leaves,
Each moment captured, the heart believes.
With every turn, a brighter light,
Guiding us gently through the night.

Hidden treasures on the way,
In laughter shared, in words we say.
Together we chase horizons wide,
In glimmers found, we find our stride.

So trust the journey, embrace the flow,
For glimmers in the turns will show.
In every twist, a story starts,
Illuminating all our hearts.

A Dance with the Unknown

In shadows deep, we start to sway,
Embracing fear in the night's ballet.
Each step we take, a whispered chance,
In this uncertain, fleeting dance.

With every twirl, the world expands,
We grasp at dreams with trembling hands.
The unknown calls, a siren's song,
In its embrace, we feel we belong.

Stars above, they guide our way,
Through night's embrace, we choose to play.
Together lost, yet never alone,
In this dance, we find our home.

So leap with me into the dark,
Where sparks ignite and futures spark.
For in this dance, let shadows meet,
And find the joy in lost retreat.

Spaces Between Steps

In quiet breaths, the pauses bloom,
Where thoughts take flight amid the gloom.
Each heartbeat echoes time's refrain,
In silence dwells a hidden gain.

We measure life in moments still,
In every space, a breath, a thrill.
From step to step, we weave our fate,
In careful dance, we contemplate.

The path ahead, a distant haze,
Yet in this space, our spirits raise.
With each small sigh, the world unfolds,
In gentle hands, our dreams we hold.

So linger long in twilight's glow,
Embrace the gaps where wonders flow.
For in these pauses, life is found,
A sacred dance on hallowed ground.

Pathways of the Heart

Through tangled trails, we walk as one,
Beneath the shadows of the sun.
Each step we take, a story shared,
In pathways where our dreams have dared.

Silent whispers guide our way,
In every choice, a chance to sway.
With every beat, our hearts align,
In winding circles, love will shine.

We trace the maps of hopes and fears,
Through laughter, pain, and joyful tears.
Each road ahead, a new desire,
In paths well-worn, we find our fire.

So hold my hand, let's journey forth,
Through streets of gold, to hidden worth.
For in the heart's embrace, we'll find,
The paths we tread, forever kind.

Wandering Thoughts

In fields of dreams, my mind will roam,
To places where my heart calls home.
Each thought a bird, it takes to flight,
In swirling skies, a pure delight.

From whispered hopes to distant lands,
I gather treasures with my hands.
In every thought, a tale to tell,
A tapestry where wonders dwell.

Yet in this wander, I often pause,
To cherish moments, to seek the cause.
With every ponder, I find my way,
In wandering thoughts, I long to stay.

So let me drift in sweet embrace,
Where dreams collide and time gives chase.
For in this realm, my spirit flies,
In wandering thoughts, the heart's sunrise.

Colors of the Adventure

In the dawn's soft light, we set our sail,
Hints of gold and crimson trail.
Starlit paths and swirling dreams,
Nature whispers, flowing streams.

Mountains rise, a canvas wide,
Colors blaze and spirits glide.
Every hue a tale to weave,
In each moment, we believe.

Fields of green and skies of blue,
Adventure calls, we venture through.
With every step, the world unfolds,
The beauty in each story told.

As dusk descends, the shadows play,
Dancing colors fade away.
Yet in our hearts, the hues remain,
A vibrant mark of joy and pain.

Wandering Spirits

The night unfolds with stars so bright,
Wandering souls in the moonlight.
Whispers carried on the breeze,
In secret places, hearts find ease.

Lost in dreams, we share our thoughts,
Time becomes what cannot be caught.
Wandering spirits, hand in hand,
Make their peace with this strange land.

Paths untaken, secrets shared,
In tangled woods, we're unprepared.
Each echo leads us ever on,
A dance of shadows till the dawn.

In every tear, a tale resides,
Wandering on with open guides.
Together, in this cosmic thread,
We find the words that have been said.

Whims of the Way

Beneath the sun, we roam and play,
Embrace the whims of the way.
Twisting paths and moments bright,
Each adventure feels so right.

Curved around the granite stones,
We dance past rivers, wild moans.
Every turn a thrill unsealed,
Life's gentle truth, our hearts revealed.

With gentle winds that shift and guide,
We chase the clouds, no shame, no pride.
The humble joys that life bestows,
In whispers soft, our spirit grows.

Winding trails beneath the trees,
Time escapes, a playful tease.
With every step, the world aligns,
In the whims of way, our heart finds.

Beneath the Canopy

Beneath the canopy, we stand,
Nature's green, a sacred land.
Leaves like whispers in the air,
Every breath a moment rare.

Birdsongs echo through the height,
Guiding us in morning light.
Hidden wonders yet to see,
Beneath the life, we feel so free.

Sunbeams dance on forest floors,
Opening ancient, wooden doors.
In every shadow, secrets gleam,
A world alive, a waking dream.

Together, lost in nature's grace,
Each heartbeat finds a sacred space.
In the whispering woods, we roam,
Beneath the canopy, we're home.

Echoes of the Unknown

Whispers travel through the night,
Carried on the wings of fright.
Secrets hide in shadows deep,
Echoes of the dreams we keep.

Footsteps fade on paths untold,
Stories waiting to unfold.
Every sound, a haunting call,
In the silence, we can fall.

Voices murmur in the air,
Clues we seek but rarely share.
Mysteries swirl, a gentle tease,
Leaving hearts with wary ease.

Bravely we tread the darkened way,
Guided by the faintest ray.
In the unknown, hope still glows,
For in the dark, true courage grows.

The Search for Synthesis

Fragmented thoughts in scattered light,
Chasing shadows, fleeing night.
In a world of clash and contrast,
We seek a union, hold it fast.

Colors blend, collide, and spin,
A tapestry of loss and win.
In harmony, we find our ground,
A symphony in silence found.

Questions linger, answers brief,
Compromise, the heart's relief.
From discord springs the greatest song,
In the balance, we belong.

Elements converge like streams,
Building dreams from fractured seams.
Together, life's complexities,
Compose a dance, a gentle breeze.

Invisible Turns

Life's a maze, a winding road,
Where hidden paths, our course erode.
Choices linger, shadows cast,
Moments fleeting, seldom last.

Each turn taken, a story spun,
In silence whispers, battles won.
Unseen forces guide the way,
Molding night into the day.

A hidden map within our hearts,
Where every journey, nature imparts.
The unseen guide, a silent friend,
Leads us forth, where dreams transcend.

In the dance of fate and time,
We learn to listen, feel the rhyme.
Every turn, a chance to grow,
In invisible paths, we flow.

Footprints in the Dust

Footprints tread on sandy ground,
Stories captured, echoes found.
Trace of life in every grain,
Memories woven in joy and pain.

As the winds of time blow strong,
Shapes and forms will fade along.
Yet each mark speaks of a life,
Of love, of loss, of daily strife.

We leave behind what once was real,
In every scar, a heart will heal.
Dust may settle, but tales revive,
In the stories that we strive.

So walk with purpose, leave your sign,
For every moment, every line.
In the dust, we etch our trust,
In footprints marked, we must adjust.

The Road Less Traveled

In the hush of dawn, I stand,
A path unfolds, not well planned.
Footsteps light on dewy grass,
A whispering breeze invites to pass.

Each twist and turn, a chance to find,
A world uncharted, undefined.
With every step, a story called,
A journey new, where dreams enthralled.

Above, the sky a canvas wide,
As hopes take flight, where fears subside.
The heart's compass, true and bold,
Guides me forth, as the day unfolds.

At last, I see the summit near,
Oh, treasured moments, crystal clear.
The road less traveled, a gift to me,
In every choice, I'm finally free.

Patterns of the Way

Each step creates a sacred dance,
A pattern formed in chance and glance.
Beneath the stars, my worries wane,
As trails intertwine like gentle rain.

The mountains rise, their shadows stretch,
Every twist, a change to fetch.
In sunlight's glow, I trace my fate,
Each moment woven, never late.

The whispers of the winds relate,
Stories of love that can't wait.
Paths converge and then diverge,
A tapestry where souls emerge.

With every twist, a lesson learned,
In laughter shared, in fires burned.
Patterns of the way unfold,
A map of life, in threads of gold.

Unraveled Journeys

In winding roads, the truths unwind,
The threads of life, so intertwined.
With every bend, a sight unseen,
Unraveled journeys, where I've been.

Through forests deep and rivers wide,
Old maps forgotten, dreams abide.
Footprints lead to hidden glades,
Where memories linger, unafraid.

The heart remembers what the eyes miss,
In silent whispers, there's a bliss.
With every choice, a story spun,
Unraveled paths, the race I run.

In twilight's glow, reflections shine,
Navigating the curve, divine.
Every journey brings me home,
To the places where I roam.

A Tapestry of Trails

On distant hills, in morning's light,
I weave my dreams, a colorful sight.
A tapestry of trails I tread,
With each new path, a thread is spread.

The world unfolds, both wide and vast,
Moments cherished, never surpassed.
Through fields of gold and forests green,
The beauty of life, forever seen.

Stories woven in the air,
With laughter shared and hearts laid bare.
In every fiber, life's embrace,
A tapestry, a sacred space.

Together we journey, hand in hand,
Creating life's most wondrous strand.
A masterpiece of love and grace,
In every trail, your heart I trace.

Echoes in the Bend

In shadows where the river flows,
Whispers of the past arise,
Softly through the willow grows,
A symphony beneath the skies.

Lingering in the dusky light,
Memories dance like fireflies,
Each echo holds a story tight,
Bound within the night's replies.

The bending path of time unwinds,
As stars begin to softly gleam,
In every turn, a truth unwinds,
A fading, yet unbroken dream.

With every ripple, every sound,
Reminders of what used to be,
In silence, lies the love we found,
Echoes wrapped in mystery.

Life's Meandering Path

Winding roads beneath the trees,
Footsteps trace the tales we've spun,
Each turn reveals the gentle breeze,
Carrying whispers of the sun.

Beneath the weight of skies so vast,
Moments slip like grains of sand,
In the stillness, fleeting past,
We gather dreams with open hands.

Meadows stretch where flowers bloom,
In colors bright and sweet delight,
Through shadows cast, beyond the gloom,
We wander forth into the light.

Each step a dance, each breath a sigh,
Life's rhythm sings in every heart,
A journey shared beneath the sky,
A masterpiece of every part.

Whispers of the Journey

Through valleys deep and mountains high,
The road unfolds with every mile,
With every laugh and every cry,
We gather strength, we learn to smile.

In quiet moments, deeply shared,
Wisdom flows like rivers wide,
In gentle whispers, hearts are bared,
As love and hope walk side by side.

The path is paved with dreams we chase,
With every detour, life reveals,
In every challenge, grace and space,
To grow, to heal, to turn the wheels.

So here we stand, in time's embrace,
With open hearts and eyes that see,
The journey's whispers, a sacred place,
Where souls entwine, forever free.

Over hills and Hollows

Over hills where shadows creep,
And hollows hold their secret song,
The journey calls, its promise deep,
    Inviting us to wander long.

With every rise, a view unfolds,
A tapestry of earth and sky,
Beneath the warmth, the sun bestows,
    A brighter path that dares to fly.

Across the valleys, echoes play,
In laughter shared, in tender sighs,
Each moment cherished, come what may,
    In nature's arms, our spirits rise.

So let us roam through heart and mind,
Embrace the unknown, take the leap,
For over hills, what's yet to find,
Awaits the brave who dare to seek.

Into the Untamed

Whispers of the wild call out,
Through tangled trails and shadows stout,
Where nature's voice sings loud and free,
Awakening the heart's decree.

Underneath the sprawling skies,
With every step, the spirit flies,
Among the trees, in secret groves,
Discovering what the wild behoves.

Rivers dance with a joyful leap,
While mountains guard their secrets deep,
In every corner, life will bloom,
A canvas bright, dispelling gloom.

Into the untamed, we shall roam,
Finding there our truest home,
In nature's arms, we lose all fears,
And treasure life throughout the years.

Swaying with the Currents

Drifting softly with the tide,
Where time and motion coincide,
Each wave a story, old and new,
Carried onward, dreams pursue.

Beneath the surface, secrets dwell,
In watery depths, a silent spell,
The dance of life, a gentle sway,
As currents chart the course of day.

Ripples whisper of the past,
Moments fleeting, memories cast,
Guided by the flow so wide,
We surrender, and in we glide.

Swaying low with the currents' grace,
Finding peace in this open space,
Together sailing, hearts aligned,
In ocean's heart, our souls entwined.

The Journey's Lament

Every path has stones to tread,
Each step a tale of dreams unsaid,
With burdens worn, we journey on,
Through twilight's haze to greet the dawn.

What once was bright now holds a sigh,
As shadows linger, memories lie,
Though weary souls may seek the light,
The road ahead is steeped in night.

Whispers of lost hopes return,
In flickered flame, the past we learn,
But hearts must carry on the strain,
Bearing weight of joy and pain.

The journey's lament soft yet clear,
Echoes through the skies we steer,
Each moment lived, a precious gift,
Through trials faced, our spirits lift.

Cracks in the Pavement

In city streets where dreams collide,
Amidst the rush, there's nowhere to hide,
Cracks in the pavement tell a tale,
Of lives like rivers that twist and sail.

Each fissure holds a glimpse of grace,
A flower blooms in confined space,
Defiant colors break the gray,
As nature finds a way to sway.

Beneath the concrete, life persists,
In every gap, a chance resisted,
Echoes of laughter, whispers of strife,
Reminders of a vibrant life.

Cracks in the pavement mark our place,
Where hope and struggle interlace,
In every step, a story grows,
Of resilience, and love that shows.

Serpentines of Solitude

In shadows deep where silence weaves,
A path unfolds, where stillness breathes.
Whispers of thoughts, like snakes that glide,
In the heart's chamber, secrets hide.

Branches sway with a mournful tune,
While murmurs dance beneath the moon.
Each turn reveals a hidden thought,
Within the solitude, battles fought.

Tangles of dreams, both sharp and sweet,
Upon the road where lost souls meet.
Search for solace on winding ways,
In the quiet, there's much to praise.

Yet in the depths of this private crawl,
Strength is found, when shadows call.
Embrace the beauty of being alone,
For in silence, true strength is grown.

Embrace the Unseen

Beyond the veil where shadows lie,
A world exists, where dreams defy.
Listen closely, the heart will know,
To see the light in what won't show.

Through misty paths, the whispers guide,
With courage built, we turn the tide.
Each step we take in faith not sight,
Transcends the darkness, brings forth light.

Hidden beauty in every sigh,
Fragments of truth that never die.
With open hearts, we journey far,
Towards unseen realms and distant stars.

In the vastness of the boundless space,
Life unfolds with unhurried grace.
Embrace the unseen, with all you've got,
For in that trust, despair is not.

Journeys Through Memory

A tapestry of yesteryears,
Threads of joy, woven with tears.
Every echo sings a tale,
In the heart's archive, dreams set sail.

Footsteps linger on familiar ground,
Voices of past in silence found.
Every moment, a precious key,
Unlocks the chambers of memory.

Through corridors of faded light,
We wander on the edge of night.
Keep the whispers safe and near,
For memories shape what we hold dear.

As paths unfold like ancient lore,
We trace our lives, forevermore.
Journeys through memory, vast and wide,
In every heartbeat, we reside.

The Uncharted Terrain

Beyond the maps, the wild calls,
In uncharted lands, adventure sprawls.
With every step, the unknown gleams,
A promise held in fervent dreams.

Mountains rise with stories untold,
Rivers whisper of paths bold.
In every leaf, in every breeze,
The spirit dances, seeks to please.

Find the trails where few will tread,
Follow the sun, let fear be shed.
In the heart of chaos, beauty sings,
Amidst the uncertainty, freedom springs.

So venture forth, let courage reign,
Explore the depths of the unknown terrain.
For life's true magic lies in the chase,
Embrace the wild with open grace.

Time's Spiral

Time circles round, a dance unseen,
Moments whisper in the spaces between.
Days blend softly, shadows grow long,
In the heart's chamber, memories belong.

Ticking clocks weave stories untold,
Echoes of laughter, the young and the old.
As seasons change, the past holds tight,
Guiding lost souls through the velvet night.

In the spiral's grip, we learn to let go,
Embracing the flow, the ebb and the glow.
Life's wondrous journey flows with the tide,
In whispers of time, we take each stride.

Counting the stars that flicker and gleam,
Chasing the echoes of every lost dream.
In the spiral's embrace, we find our way,
Carving new paths into the brightening day.

Unfurling the Map

Beneath the sky, a parchment spreads wide,
With rivers of ink where secrets abide.
Mountains rise tall in a dance of the brave,
While whispers of travelers flow like a wave.

Each line a journey, each mark a tale,
Adventures await, where the heart sets sail.
With compass in hand, we chase the unknown,
Finding our way, together, alone.

In corners of wonder, the wild winds blow,
With every new turn, possibilities grow.
A treasure of moments, waiting to find,
The map is our canvas, the world, unconfined.

Unfurling the map, we fold in the dreams,
Charting our course through starlit gleams.
No boundaries now, as horizons extend,
Every step forward, a story to mend.

A Canvas of Footprints

In the sand, where the waves leave their mark,
A story unfolds, igniting the spark.
Footprints dance lightly, a fleeting embrace,
Echoes of laughter, a time, a place.

Each step an impression, a moment that glows,
The tide ebbs and flows, but the memory grows.
Beneath the vast sky, our paths intertwine,
With colors of evening, our souls align.

A gallery opened, the heart is the muse,
In whispers of breezes, we dare to choose.
Moments like brushstrokes, with purpose, they blend,
Each footprint a story, a journey, a friend.

On this canvas of life, we walk hand in hand,
Crafting our tales on the shores of the sand.
Every impression, a dance in the light,
In the canvas of footprints, our spirits take flight.

Milton Keynes UK
Ingram Content Group UK Ltd.
UKHW022005131124
451149UK00013B/1020

9 789916 908273